Great Taste ~ Low Fat

GRILLING

TIME
LIFE
BOOKS

ALEXANDRIA, VIRGINIA

TABLE OF CONTENTS

Salmon Steaks with Pesto and Peppers

page 99

Vegetables

Desserts

INTRODUCTION

Grilling's soaring popularity shouldn't be surprising; countless delicious meals can be cooked with ease in the great outdoors while enjoying summer's long, languorous evenings. It's the best way to keep the kitchen cool in hot weather—and even the finest kitchen range can't duplicate the uniquely savory, smoky flavors of foods grilled over a fire. Gas grills make outdoor cooking a snap, and you don't even need to wait for warm weather to use them.

There used to be just two choices for the classic cookout: Hot dogs or hamburgers. Toasted marshmallows served as dessert. Today, there's much more to choose from, and fat-laden hot dogs will soon be a thing of the past when you have this book in hand: It's a treasure trove of innovative grilling ideas for meat, poultry, seafood, vegetables, and even desserts. Our chefs have come up with superb original recipes that feature surprising tricks for healthful, high-flavor grilling. Some entrées even have built-in grilled side dishes for the simplest meals ever.

SOMETHING FOR EVERYONE

The ever-popular chicken appears here in many guises. Our Poultry chapter will ensure that you never get bored with birds. Flavor-packed marinades take the place of sticky sauces, and poultry can be grilled with the skin to keep it moist. (As long as you discard the skin before eating, the fat is out of the picture.) There are succulent barbecues as well as festive salads; the Charcoal-Grilled Turkey Breast with Stuffing makes a fabulous nontraditional holiday meal.

You needn't deprive yourself of meat on the grill. The following luscious entrées (among others) are satisfying *and* low in fat: Marinated Flank Steak and Potato Salad, Moroccan Lamb Kebabs, and Beef Burgers with Basil and Mozzarella.

Delicate fish and shellfish may seem challenging candidates for grilling, but a grill-topper or grilling basket makes striped bass or scallops as easy to cook as steaks or chops, with spectacular results. The Seafood chapter includes recipes for swordfish and tuna—the two meatiest, easiest-to-handle fish—but don't hesitate to try Jamaican Jerked Shrimp with Pineapple or Grilled Scallops with Thai Noodle Salad as well.

These days we're all trying to eat more vegetables and less meat. Open to our Vegetables chapter (and welcome vegetarian friends) with such hearty dishes as Grilled Vegetable and Mozzarella Sandwiches, Grilled Pizza, or Vegetable Burritos. You'll also find pleasing "side orders" in this chapter, from colorful vegetable kebabs to classic grilled